3 9635 1034 8902 9

D1571251

73

Redhead and the Slaughter King

ଔ

by Megan Falley

Write Bloody Publishing
America's Independent Press

Austin, TX

WRITEBLOODY.COM

Redhead and the Slaughter King

© 2014 Megan Falley

No part of this book may be used or performed without written consent from the author, except for critical articles or reviews.

Write Bloody
First Edition
ISBN: 978-1938912450

Cover art by Ashley Siebels
Proofread by Miles Walser
Edited by Heather Knox, Sean Patrick Mulroy, Jared Singer, Jeanann Verlee, & Miles Walser
Author Photo by Bridget Badore
Interior layout by Ashley Siebels

Type set in Bergamo from www.theleagueofmoveabletype.com

Printed in Tennessee, USA

Write Bloody Publishing
Austin, TX
Support Independent Presses
writebloody.com

To contact the author, send an email to writebloody@gmail.com

MADE IN THE USA

REDHEAD AND THE SLAUGHTER KING

for Sean, for choosing life.

REDHEAD
AND THE
SLAUGHTER KING

V.

IV.

III.

II.

I.

V.

BACKHANDED APOLOGY

I am sorry I am woman. Sorry for the cicadas of my chest, how they hibernated for thirteen years, then ruined your summer. Sorry for each freckle on my shoulder—specks of dirt in your pancake batter. Sorry the high school banned tank tops so you could concentrate on your math. Sorry I bled on your couch. Sorry I didn't tell you, flipped the cushion upside-down. Sorry I grow hair, like you. Sorry that even in television commercials for women's razors it's always a bare, bronzed leg being shaved. Sorry I'm not already all the way removed. Sorry for walking down the street wearing that skirt. Sorry for the minutes it took out of your workday to gawk like that. To say those things. Sorry I didn't say, *Thank you.* I thought you were going to kill me. Sorry I keep my mail, front door, and apartment key between each of my fingers when I walk. Sorry I say sorry so much. Sorry you got fired for grabbing my ass like it was the candy on my desk. Of course it belonged to you. Sorry for all the ridiculous laws—of gravity too—I'm sure my breasts are very happy to see you. Sorry you liked breast milk so much. Sorry I fed you in public and let everyone know you loved a woman then. Sorry I was your first home and didn't leave my body open for you to crawl back in. Sorry that the egg that made me came from inside my mother when she was inside her mother. Sorry for all this forever. Sorry you're on the outside of the joke. Sorry I bled on your couch and I didn't turn over the cushion this time.

THE SUIT

The suit was probably a hand-me-down from my brother,
and I'm not sure where I got the briefcase, or the shoes,
but the baseball cap was my own: a relic from the years
I spent trying to be a trophy for my father's shelf and failing.
Benched by my own dad.

The other girls were what they always were:
fairies, Barbies, princesses and dolls, some babies
for the third year in a row. But I didn't want to be
something so helpless, so kitten.

I pressed the stick-on mustache above my lip
and ran my finger along it, remembered the time
my brother cried because dad shaved his off —
he didn't recognize him without the furry badge
that made him father.

I'm not sure if I shoved a sock in my underwear
or not, but I walked like I had,
like I inherited the earth.

The other boys tried to one-up each other
with who had the most muscle: the cop,
the Power Ranger, the ninja, the shark.

But I knew, as they had taught me in school,
as life would constantly remind me—a ribbon
wrapped around my finger so tightly it draws blood—
I was the most powerful thing I could be. I was a man.

I didn't ask for the candy with a curtsy or a *please.*
I jabbed my hand into the bowl.
I took.

ALIBI

for the rapist who used the excuse of sexsomnia to clear his name

I've suddenly contracted a sleep-punching disease.
I'm going to cuddle up next to everyone
who believes your shit.

In my disease
I tie balloon animals
out of scrotums.

It's okay. I'm sleeping.
I don't want to be held
accountable either.

It's funny, your disease
manifested itself at thirty-one years old
when you had a beautiful woman in your bed.

Curious it didn't haunt you
on your camping trip
with Grandpa.

If I had an affliction where I unconsciously shoved
a pistol into the mouths of people I loved,
I'd tell them,

Look, I do this thing
in the night—it might kill you,
but it isn't me.

Except
I'd know
it *was*.

I'd sleep in a crypt.
I'd cut off
my own hands.

TELLING HIM I KISSED A WOMAN

I cut the pill of truth
with honey, promised,

We were drunk.

Said we were egged on
by barstools, wore dresses of gin.

Said I stumbled
onto her face, more so
than an actual kiss.

Spun it as if cameras
were rolling, an image he could beat
off to instead of curse. Said,

It meant nothing.

And how could it?
I was straight
as a wedding aisle.

I touched his beard.
Begged him to stay.
Insisted,

It was only a kiss,

and hoped he wouldn't hear it
in my voice, how it sounded like,

It was only a decade.
It was only a war.

I didn't tell him
there was no bar,
no audience

except the magnetic poetry tiles
falling to the floor as she pressed me
against the refrigerator, beaming.

I did not say I felt more in that
one kiss than anytime he thrust
his tongue down my throat,

or wouldn't get a condom,
or wanted it facedown.
Swore instead,

It will never happen again.

He called me a whore.
I said,

I love you.

He called me a bitch.
I said,

Yes.

Letter from the First Woman I Tried to Love

I promised myself if I won the staring contest,
I would kiss you. But I blinked first,
and kissed you anyway.

The mosquitos were lucky we were shy
in that garden, they feasted on the two girls
pretending not to know why they were there.
They liked your blood better.

I knew you were out of my league
but you threw me the ball all summer.
Was it because you knew
I couldn't hurt you?

Because I had air-conditioning
and a first-aid kit and a guitar I could make sing
your name like a rescued dog?

You always showed up with a bottle of wine
or honey whiskey and it took me too long
to see you needed to be drunk
to touch or be touched.

I tried not to let it kill me,
which I learned from watching you,
you who licked the salt from your wounds
and sucked down tequila. Your own mouth,
a lime.

But in the morning you'd apologize
by driving me to the river, or splitting
an avocado and giving me
the bigger half,

and I told myself you'd learn
to love me, and I never forgave you
for how close you might have come

if we had met in a different year,
in different bodies.

I think there's a difference
between being a bad person
and being bad at being a person,

and I think you know
which one you are.

Conditional Statement

*to the woman who said, "Drop the restraining order,
don't jeopardize his freedom."*

If I didn't ask my father to carry me
to that courthouse where I spent the morning
filling out paperwork amongst bruised women
and their crawling daughters

If I didn't spend the afternoon
there, braiding my own spine

If I didn't stand beside the man I once called
Home and *Honey,* place my shaking hand
beside his grubby one on that Bible
where thousands of atheists had sworn
before—no more than good fiction

If I didn't keep a piece of paper
folded in my wallet at all times,
an electric fence protecting me
from a dog known to bite

If I didn't call the cops
when the dog ripped through the currents
and shocks of that fence, my skirt
the only flavor on the mind of his teeth

If I didn't put his face on all those posters

If I didn't say his name again and again
like a fable told to girls

If I did what they told me to do—
found a different scene, a different state,
a new number, a new name

If, instead, I swallowed
the gasoline, put that first match out
on my obedient tongue

If I stayed small,
shoved my hands into apron pockets
and my head into an oven—which was,
maybe, the easier way—

then there would be more of us.

CINNAMON AND SAND

You have woken up
on a sliver of his king-sized bed
every day for a year.

This morning,
you let him make love
to you—five times.

You are thinking
of adding vanilla extract
to his pancake batter,

of arranging blueberries on his plate
in the shape of your names.
Of the places outside his big city window

he has not yet paraded you through.
There are still barstools in this borough
that don't know you're *his* girl.

You point to the shower, the doorknob,
to last night's stripped-off clothing
begging for your bodies to fill them,

the day that darkens so fast.

When you inch out of bed
he asks, *Where do you think
you're going?*

The story does not change.

He has never,
and will not now
snatch your wrist.

Will not pin, force,
will not smack
from you a chorus of yeses.

You are a girl.
You have learned
to bargain with laughter before.

But this morning your giggle
is a foreign currency
he will not accept.

You explain the wound
between your legs. How the well has dried up.
Feels like thick cotton rags folded inside you.

The story does not change.

He does not yank you
by the braids. There is no hand
wrapped like duct tape around your mouth—

there never was and there won't be now.

Instead, he charms the guilt from your hips.
Says you are a feast and he, the famine.
How selfish it would be to hoard such fruit.

You explain a second time—fat cotton rags
folded inside. Dry as licking cinnamon and sand.
Pain, you say. *A small rip.*

He does not claw
open your dress.
Rather, he says,

If our appetites don't align,
we probably will not work.

You whimper, beg, say, *Five times*
already this morning, Baby. Wound. Rip.
Cinnamon and sand. He says,

Probably will not work.

He doesn't lift a finger,
but smirks as you throw yourself down.
Pin your own shoulders back.

Split your favorite dress
on purpose.
Rip.

THE BALANCE

after Rachel McKibbens

There were days when it looked like love.
Bus rides asleep on each other's shoulders,

splitting a pair of earbuds.
Afternoons where we stayed in

our pajamas and played video games
after he bought us twin bodega sandwiches

and remembered mine
without meat.

And while I look back on these memories
with equal, if not more repulsion,

I know I wasn't an idiot to stay—
that my heart invented its own verb

which meant *to love the dog
who licks the scar it gave you.*

On a dirty bar couch on Valentine's Day
he said, *I would fight with you every morning*

if it meant I could kiss you every night, and at the time
it didn't sound like the Codependent National Anthem

or a vending machine where you put in fury
and get out passion,

or even like the things I read now in pamphlets—
the ones I thrust upon others like my own righteous gospel.

It sounded like the sweetest thing
he'd ever say to me. A poem

I could fold up small and carry around
in my locket, not noticing, for months,

how it choked.

A GENTLEMAN'S AGREEMENT

The court requires a fee to have a subpoena served by a professional.
However, a friend or family member can deliver it (for a different kind of cost).

I.

My family and I circle around a table
to stare down the paper laid out before us—
a roast too bloody to eat.

We debate over who should deliver
the court-ordered wall to keep a man
I trusted from entering unwanted.

We decide it shouldn't be my mother—
we know how he treats women.
I think my brother is the obvious choice,

looks most like a prison guard.
His eager knuckles are chalk-outline white;
his hands, boulders for the stoning.

Mom says we don't want two court dates,
so we choose my father: harmless as a cartoon,
everybody's tie-dyed pal.

II.

The apartment door was open
so my father let himself in

like an old friend. Shook his hand
as if agreeing on a dowry.

I will never forgive that hand
for belonging to a gentleman.

For being a palm
instead of a sledgehammer.

RETRACTION TO
"A GENTLEMAN'S AGREEMENT"

My father is the champion
of getting out of parking tickets.
He is every traffic cop's nightmare.

Once, he held up a ticket to the judge
as if it were the winning lotto numbers,
pointed to where it read, PRINT NAME CLEARLY,

and then to the policeman's harried signature.
I can't read that—can you, Your Honor?
he asked. *I can't*, said the Judge,

who ruled the ticket defective.
He was even excused from smashing
the top of a taxi with a baseball bat

when he saw a cabbie
refusing to release
the young woman inside.

You always tell us if we see somethin',
say somethin'. Now tell me—what if
it had been your daughter?

My dad clobbered that car
before I was born, but I like to pretend
he saw me in the taxi.

I like to watch
the baseball bat
crashing down.

IV.

WATCHING MY MOTHER IN THE MIRROR

First, she finds out the preference of the man she's seeing
that night—blondes or brunettes—becomes the woman on the box.

Most often she's a redhead, or is it *Light Auburn,*
True Pomegranate, Number 4RR?

She blow-dries her hair upside-down,
and every time she flips over she's a new version of my mom,

a rose that keeps blooming
into a different shade of itself.

If the man of the night is a lawyer, she will rub
her wrists and the nape of her neck with money.

If he's a doctor, she will prick her finger
with a sewing needle and dab a fresh glow on her cheeks.

It seems I'm always zipping her
into a new dress.

⟼

I'm the only girl in school (whose mother isn't dead)
who doesn't know how to braid her own hair.
But I know how to take a *whore's bath*

which is what mom calls a quick rinse
in just a few inches of water, some rose soap
scrubbed under your armpits and crotch.

I know how to shave hair that hasn't grown in yet.
I know you don't have to wear panties
with tights. I know that if you hold a match

to an eyeliner pencil,
it goes on smooth
as a lie.

⊢

The boy has a girlfriend who isn't me and I say, *okay*. The boy says he
just wants to be friends with benefits and I say, *me too*. The boy says
he thinks it's *really cool* that my mom doesn't care if he sleeps in my
bed even though he's nine years older. The boy promises he will let
me know before he comes, but never does. The boy laughs when I call
him an asshole. The boy calls me a bitch and I stay. *Good dog.*

⊢

Did you know that women kill themselves
in prettier ways than men?
While a man might open his face
with a shotgun, a woman prefers the wrists.
A woman is always a portrait
of pills. Gasoline filling up in the garage
as if waiting for you
to take her for a ride.

⊢

My love
sits at the foot of my bed,
crying.

The doctors told him
it might be serious,
to wait a week

for the blood results.
To avoid sex
in the meantime.

My love, he loves me.
I know because he's warning me,
and because of how he holds me—

like if I tried to let go,
he wouldn't
pull harder.

And I know I love him too
because I reach for his belt
and begin unbuckling.

I know he won't find another woman
who loves like this, the way my mother
taught me how.

TUTOR

At fifteen, the boys started whistling
me out of my bedroom window.
I didn't ask my mother

before shaving my legs. I bloodied
the shower curtain and left
it for her to clean.

I learned that replacing vodka with water
only worked if you didn't freeze it—
how easy it was to lie.

My first real boyfriend was a college guy who drove
five hours downstate to be there for me
and my first blowjob.

I didn't have a bedroom
to bring him to. Mine was still pink
with shame. An audience of dolls.

My mother would try
to pay him, assuming
he was my math tutor.

We drove a while, looking for a spot to park.
Finally—the vacant lot of my elementary school.
The seats in back of his van already shoved down.

Nothing to say,
no flavor left
in my gum,

I spidered my mouth along his
stomach, hairy, like my father's,
and tried to remember

locker room advice, magazine tips,
the blocked channels—but they never told me
he'd help.

He'd be the carriage driver
and the prince. Me—his horse.
My hair—his reins.

When he kissed my forehead after,
I knew I'd passed. Knew it was silly
to have been afraid.

I asked him not to drive me home,
to let me out there. And I wandered
my old playground,

swung my old swings,
and thought, how *lucky* I was.
What a woman I would be.

CUTTING SCHOOL

after Joshua Marie Wilkinson

One girl runs out of the classroom when the health teacher pops a tape into the VCR about anorexia. One girl tells the foreign exchange student to *buy some fucking deodorant.* One girl bakes in the tanning salon so often she burns a crater into her face. One girl carves her boyfriend's initials into her arm with a paperclip and starts a trend. One girl still doesn't know she smoked oregano. One girl pulls her thong up above her pants and bends over at her bottom locker. One girl tells her lab partner to have fun on the roller coasters during the physics field trip, *it's okay*, she'll do all the work. One girl sends a valentine to herself. One girl changes into her gym clothes in the bathroom stall every day. One girl has a hundred bracelets up her arms. One girl rips down her own student council campaign poster when she sees what was drawn on her mouth. One girl spent the summer finally growing breasts and the rest of the school year trying to cut them off.

Ashley Handler Doesn't Walk, She Floats

Birds hang Ashley Handler's laundry.
She is the State Flower of Long Island.
Ashley Handler sits next to me in chorus class
and I hope there's scientific evidence of girls like me
becoming pretty through osmosis.

Ashley Handler was drinking with friends
when she floated across Sunrise Highway.
She was struck by a car, her body
carried away by birds (EMTs).

Ashley Handler's rib poked through her lung
as if the lung was a doorbell and the rib
was a finger, asking her heart to prom.

Both Ashley Handler's clavicles were broken,
and the birds worried,
From where will we drink?

It is cool to visit Ashley Handler in the hospital.
I bring her a few word searches and crossword puzzles
I handmade for her. I made the answers
things I thought she'd like: puppies, lip gloss.

Ashley Handler doesn't wear make-up
with her hospital gown. Seeing her
without it is like undressing
the tinsel from Christmas and suddenly
there is nothing more beautiful
than a simple tree.

Here, the boys come, bring bouquets
of jokes and charm. They hope
she is a hatching chick—that she will follow
them forever if they just happen to be there
the next time she opens her eyes.

When she does, finally, open them,
all she asks for
is a mirror.

Ashley Handler returns to school
in a wheelchair. She's allowed to leave class
five minutes early to avoid the bustle
of the hall. She can choose any friend
to help carry her books.

It isn't getting out of class
that makes the hands of the entire room
shoot up like eager flowers, desperate
to be picked—

it is her. It is the chance
to glide beside her, slow.
It is the empty hallway,

and hoping, in the quiet
of it, she will lift up her shirt
and show us
her scars.

What We Lose

I. The Skinny Girls at Fat Camp

Jenny wasn't back in time for lights out.
Our counselors went searching for her, assuming
she'd left her lips inside a boy's bunk.
Instead, they found her sharpening her hipbones
around the track. Us girls all angry
for not thinking of it first.

That week, after weigh-ins,
I consoled my best friend, an 86-pound teenager,
by holding up a slab of gray meat, swearing,
*This is what a pound looks like. If you only
lost .8 of that, it's still less of your body.*

No one sent me there. I chose
to spend five summer birthdays
disappearing. Instead of a cake,
the dining hall sang to me
as I wished on an apple
with a candle in it.

II. Alice Leaves Wonderland to Attend Her First Overeaters Anonymous Meeting

*Hi, my name is Alice, and I am an overeater. All food says, EAT ME. I am so big
that my arms and legs shoot out the windows. I ruin the house. I want to be
small enough to slip through the keyhole. I want to walk through flowers, be
mistaken for one.*

III. Fifth Grade Report Card

It was the first year they recorded our height
and weight next to our grades. I got straight A's,
but knew I was failing.

When they sent home the class photo,
I stuck a pushpin
through my own face.

THE DISCIPLES

That year we found ourselves
at the hockey rink watching the boys
skate and shoot and try not to lose
those smiles we doodled in the margins
of our notebooks during classes
we knew we'd never learn anything in.
But out there, on the periphery of ice,
we learned how to be almost-women,
how to turn A cups into cleavage,
how to twist our limp hair into wild curls.
How to wear next to nothing
all winter. We learned that some days
they'd wave, or wink, or blow
a kiss and some days
they'd pretend we didn't exist.
We never learned
the formula for why.
But we learned that we could watch
the boys, shout their names
from the sidelines,
illuminated pre-teen marquees,
but we'd be stupid to think
they'd show up to our recitals
or school plays or—hell—
even our funerals.

SAFELIGHT

The only place I loved in that school
made of algorithms and locker rooms,
bulimia and cage desks,
was the darkroom.

My first time inside I was awoken
by its red, the shade a flashlight made
pressed against my own fleshy hand.

I wanted to take off
my clothes in that darkroom,
for someone to lift me onto the counter,
cover my mouth and enter
my still-developing body.

For a boy to hold
my self-portrait in the chemical bath
until every flaw and freckle
bloomed.

For him to say, *It's beautiful,*
before laying the photo down
into the stop bath.

For me
to say, *It is.*
I am.
I know.

K

In the summer, girls lined up for her
to shave their heads on her front porch.

I sat behind her in poetry class
and when she wrote, the naked lady
tattooed on her arm writhed.
I tried to name the shade of her hair—
so black it was blue.

She loved Bukowski. Hated herself
in the most beautiful ways—pierced
five or six holes in her face.

One day in class she stole my phone,
punched her number in and saved her name—"k".
She owned ½₆ of the alphabet.

I read her messages over and over.
They were the first poems.
They were cave paintings.
They were my own palms.

The only time she ever called was 3AM.
I WANT TO KISS YOU RIGHT NOW, said her whiskey.
Don't worry, that's just something she tells new friends,
said her sober roommate, snatching the phone.

The world had never given me
the language to say, *Yes*, or, *I don't know
how to kiss you—let me kiss you,*

so I danced with a boy that night. He was tall,
I think. I slept beside him, not touching. I forgot
his name. But I remembered her

bruise-colored hair. How the dye left a spot
behind her ear. How it ruined nothing
but me.

THE BRICK HOUSE ON DAMSON LANE WITH THE RED DOOR AND ALL THE LIGHTS ON

When my mom got herself a boyfriend
and started sleeping out and leaving
for long vacations two or three times a year,
I became Queen of the House Parties.

People who used to tease me,
call me *Fat Camp* or *J.A.P.,*
were suddenly begging
to tie my shoelaces.

Still, they weren't invited. I held my grudges
the way one holds an infant.
Cooed at them and made silly faces,
proud to be their mother.

My friends helped me turn my mom's studio
into a beer pong arena. Sometimes I played
with the boys. The drunker I was, the more shots
I sank. I sank a lot of shots.

House rules were that losers had to remove
an article of clothing. You'd think I'd be timid, take off
my socks or belt first, but no. I ran my tongue
along the lip of a red cup.

The kitchen was the dance floor and we all banged
our crotches together, called it grinding,
the white kids singing every lyric
to Biggie Smalls' *Juicy.*

My bedroom became a hotbox
while the stoners ripped bongs and played
Hotel California on instruments they carried
to the party on their backs.

An *Elevator Shotty* was when one person stuck
the lit end of a blunt in their mouth and blew an ejaculation
of smoke into another person's, lips close
as a kiss, as they rose from crouching to standing.

The boys cheered when it was two girls.
I'd fall onto my bed with some guy's face
pushed into mine as the party dizzied
around us.

Whenever a group of kids came to my porch
begging to be let in, hoping I'd had the drink
that would make me forgiving, I crossed my arms,
shook my head, said, *Sorry, party is full,*

and closed the door on their sucker faces.
Everyone else's parents were still together,
sitting on their couches and watching bad TV
while my mom was in St. Thomas or Vancouver or Barbados

and this made me special.
When she'd come home, sunburned
and hungover, the house a perfect replica
of the way it was when she left it,

she'd find a glass shard or a sticky spot
on the floor and grill me, or ground me,
as if I didn't know how to sneak out
through every window. As if she was still my mother.

THE YEAR YOU DIED

for Anderson Yeh

The year you died, all our bicycles were stolen. All our parents split up. Some boys made fun of other boys for crying. We stopped calling the woods behind our houses *Farfignugenville*. The trees became just trees. We renamed it *The Path*. That's where we learned to drink. To drink more. We bought beer with stolen IDs and didn't make eye contact with your parents in the checkout line. No matter how many times we mopped the floor after a party it was always dirty. Everything, dirty. It was all dare and no truth. We all fucked each other. Woke up naked wrapped in paper towels on our neighbor's lawn. Called each other *retard*, *faggot*. Our college acceptance letters arrived like getaway cars. Before we left we found ourselves at your grave, wanting to leave something behind. All we had were rolling papers, condom wrappers—souvenirs of a life you'd never see. That night, we made sure we all walked each other home. The moonlight made our shadows small, like children.

Retraction To "The Year You Died"

For months we'd watch your father
at the gates after school, waiting
for a face that never came.
Halloween was hardest—little ghosts
ringing your parents' bell
as if sweetness still lived there.
If you had bullied death,
you might have a mustache by now.
Might love a girl who rolled
up her skirt before school.
Might steal your mother's car.
Our parents are fed up
with our misbehaving,
punish us for sneaking
lovers into bed, for smoking
out the window. I pierced
my bellybutton and my father
said, *I'll kill you.*

THE MERMAID'S DAUGHTER

It's true, sometimes she would comb her hair with a fork
at the dinner table rather than actually eat. Sometimes
she would bathe a whole day. Sometimes I caught her
whispering to the goldfish, but mostly she was a regular mom.
She drove me to swimming lessons and went to the movies
and criticized herself in mirrors so I would learn to do it too.
Even after she cut herself loose from the net of her marriage—
we never spoke of the deal she made to fishhook my father into love.
She got her voice back, but still—when she started dating again,
I watched her catch new men
the old way.

III.

GOLDEN BOY

My brother's hair
looked like someone cooked a porridge
comprised entirely of sunshine
and poured the bowl over his head.

It was a yellow traffic light
that everyone slowed down for.
They complimented my mother,
told her she was *lucky*.

He was a dandelion of a boy

but when we picked him up after his first day
of High School—he demanded we take him
to the barbershop.

> This memory comes before heroin
> became a household name. Before I found
> my piggybank slaughtered—my brother's mouth
> filled with more pills than teeth.

He slammed the door as he stormed
into the $7 barber. *Alone,* he growled.

I was six years old and did not know
what this meant, but I saw my mother's eyes
in the rearview mirror—she knew
what happened when dandelion boys asked
for the lawnmower.

He returned to the passenger side
years older than he was when he left it,
switched

the channel on the radio to something
harder, faster, twisted the volume knob up
to drown the words no one was speaking.

Back in the barbershop,
someone swept up
that gold-spun miracle
and threw it away.

My mother knew a war
was going to come, the way animals know
before rain. The way they know,

but can do nothing
to stop it.

ANYTHING FOR YOU

The night you called, begging
for cash, you revealed all
mom's hiding spots: a box
of calcium chews above the microwave,
a corked jar marked Unconditional Love,
between the pages of Flannery O'Connor's
A Good Man Is Hard to Find.

It's for a friend, you said.

I stole $40 from her and ran
to the mailbox—cocooned it in a letter
I pretended you would read. Soon I learned
exactly how much you would do
for that *friend.*

The best grades of your college career
came the semester you told all your teachers
mom had died.

And she did a little.

THE FIRST CEREMONY

after Natalie Diaz

If I was the family florist, I'd be responsible
for the apology of lilies.

If I was the lawyer, I'd be expected to pay
for it all—the party of black.

If I was the chef, they'd ask me to feed
those who cannot imagine eating.

But I am the writer—not the star
of the funeral, but its narrator—

here to translate the language of grief
into simple, digestible metaphor.

To wield euphemisms. Turn *addiction*
into *grip on reality*. Turn *overdose*

into *sudden, unfair.* My mother can melt
like a satin witch into her corner of the pew,

my father can do what men do: prove
his strength, become a pallbearer.

But I'm the emcee at my brother's last big party—
so I recite his eulogy

to shampoo bottles, haven't sung
in the shower for years.

My brother bangs
on the bathroom door,

says, *Hurry up—the fuck
is taking so long?*

I do hurry up.
I want him to love me.

There's still dirt on my skin, though.
There's still soap in my hair.

THE SECOND CEREMONY

We bury him with his baseball cards
because that's what he has left,
what his life amounted to. The electronics sold.
The house turned to soot at the whim of one cigarette.
Even the girls figured him out.

We bury him with his friends
outside the funeral home, too scared
to enter, sweating like burned spoons.
We replace his face in its forever bed with each of theirs,
their pockmarked arms and rotted smiles.

We bargain with the god of too late.
We bury him in his father's suit, which was too big
for him before and ridiculous now, but nobody
buys a new suit for the dead. We leave him
to lie in his potential.

I bury him with a picture of me. Don't bother
to tape the jagged, toothy edge back together.
He ripped himself out on purpose—and look
how I'm smiling in the photo. Look
how I'm leaning   on nothing.

THE THIRD CEREMONY

I am the only one at your funeral.

I fill the vase with the right flowers and press my face
into them, but only smell your cigarettes.

I recite the obituary that I've been saving for this occasion

ever since the summer you started putting fireflies
on your tongue and winning contests for cruelest hands.

I admit, it's a flawless performance, gifted to an empty room,

but I can't help but hate you for not cracking
an embalmed smirk during the funny parts.

I carry your casket alone

which is also an exercise
I've been training for.

The hearse is the only one waiting for me to finish.

There will be no procession,
no cars following behind.

You've left no shadow.

Pawned all the people who could have been here
for highs even you knew weren't worth it.

I am relieved—the worst is over.

I received the phone call,
confirmed your body.

I open a black umbrella, blame you for the rain.

MY BIGGEST FEAR FOR YOU

the prize goldfish
   are midnight–swimming
      through your powdered
         sugar veins.

carousel ponies peel
   their plastic hooves,
      kneel beside you. cold snouts
         to your colder cheek.

the bearded lady
   has the voice of our mother,
      the scruff of a policeman's
         backhand.

the kissing booth girl
   is your first & only love, undressed
      in the dunk tank,
         yoo-hooing you over.

you are married
   to cement.
      you are spinning
         everything that hurts

into cotton candy.
   whipping it all into sweet
      pink clouds that dissolve
         on your tongue.

the ferris wheel twists
   into a clock. *wake up.*
      a talking clock. *wake up. hey.*
         buddy, buddy, wake up.

the cola in your veins turns flat.
   the prize goldfish are hooked
      by the cheek with heaven's
         hungry bait.

the girl in the dunk tank
   turns blue. the carousel
      song, now a siren.
         you are carried away

into an ambulance
   the way our father
      used to carry you,
         out of the backseat

      after a long drive,
   only sleeping.

Retraction To
"My Biggest Fear for You"

~~the cop car taking you away.~~
~~the ambulance.~~

~~the relapse~~
~~or relapse again.~~

~~that you'll shoot~~
~~it this time, your arm~~
~~a thicket of black roses.~~

~~that I'll find you.~~
~~that I won't.~~
~~that the stream by our house~~
~~will, purple and wrinkled.~~

~~that you will only ever be~~
~~the sum of your habit~~
~~my brother, white powder.~~

~~that the experts were wrong~~
~~when they told our parents it wasn't their son~~
~~doing those awful things, but your addiction~~
~~acting out.~~

~~that when you call me~~
~~bitch, cunt, throw the plate across the room—~~
~~your eyes are clear. your veins too.~~
~~you're clean, sober. it isn't~~
~~the high.~~ it's

you.

PORTRAIT OF MY BROTHER AS THE TREE

Somehow, a Christmas tree limp on the curb
looks more unnatural than it does lit up
in a living room like a drunk prom queen.

Inside, a tree means laughing and carols.
Outside, it means everything we loved about winter
is gone except the cold.

So when you arrive—empty-handed
for the forevereth year in a row, humming
some dumb incandescent tune, toppling over

onto our mother, flammable—I don't kick you
to the gutter. I feed you water.
I stand you straight against the corner.

I don't care if you won't come down
until February, shedding
your needles.

I know you're just a symbol,
but it wouldn't be Christmas
without you.

Prayer for the Woman Who Will Marry My Brother

May you be the kind of woman
who can turn wine into water.

May your laugh be sparkling
cider. May you put him to bed early

on New Year's Eve and wake him
with the same resolution: *don't*

don't don't. You don't need to be a linguist,
but learn to speak his silences.

Know the subtle differences
in how he shuts a door. Or when *I'm fine*

means he's fine—and when to call
the fire department. Know the burn

before the twigs even spark.
And if you lose your way, ask me.

I am fluent. I have studied this language
my whole, wasted life.

AN APOLOGY TO MY BROTHER

I'm sorry I spill your secrets like an overfull goblet of wine. I'm sorry I think they're *mineminemine*. I'm sorry that I love you the way a shadow loves its body—that I always sniff your hair. I'm sorry that in the poems I name you *Needle*. In the poems I name you *Pill*. I'm sorry it's always *recovering*, never *recovered*. That I'm still nervous when you call. That I think it's for bail. I'm sorry that when you say *I love you* I wait for the *but*. I'm sorry I always write about you as if you are dead. It's just—I spent so many years preparing for that funeral. All my dresses are black.

THE LAST CEREMONY

The widest church in town is still
too small to fit everyone who has loved you
through its heavy doors, so we hold two funerals.

No one wears black.

We wear your sports jerseys from high school.
We wear the t-shirts you collected from the marathons
you ran to raise awareness for addiction.

Your grandchildren wear the sheets
from the forts you built with them,
cut into capes.

Your wife does not cry, she feels lucky
to have loved you. You live on in every wrinkle.
You gave her those smile lines she wears like jewelry.

The men from the meetings tell stories about you
saving them, yanking them from their own syringes
and vomit, they name their kids after you.

There are so many boys named Sean, Sean.

I wish our father was here to see this, but maybe
he's waiting up there with a catcher's mitt, maybe
there's a baseball whizzing through the air for you.

I know you'll catch it.

In the casket,
you are older than rain,
just as exquisite.

There is not a shadow
of pain on your face. You learned
the science of turning it to joy.

I remember the day,
decades ago, when you told me
I was your best friend.

I could have died right then,
but we were given the gift
of years, and dinners, and holidays,

and children, and forgiveness—
which is sweeter
than any liquor.

This is the first of your funerals
where no one asks me to make the speech.
I just sit in the front row and weep,

and am not sad.
I am the least sad
I have ever been.

II.

Dinner with Symbolism

The crucifix arrives wearing her usual:
stained pants and ratty sneakers she can't afford
to replace. She brought a platter of exotic fruit,
pistachio and rosewater cupcakes.

I don't ask how she paid for the desserts,
but make a note to recount my sock drawer bank.
She asks if I need help in the kitchen
but she's pretty useless with her hands

pinned to the cross like that.
So I tell her, *It's okay, just talk to me,*
and she tells me what all the pills
in her purse are for.

The oversized carnival teddy bear arrives
wearing a tie-dye shirt and shorts
even though it's the middle of winter.
He tells me the same stupid joke and I laugh

the same stupid laugh.
We've been doing this for years.
He gifts me a mug that reads *Baby Bear*
and I thank him, even though I'm not a bear.

Of course, we're waiting
for my brother to arrive.
He always wears a different face,
if he shows up at all.

Sometimes he is one of those
wind-up chattering teeth toys.
Sometimes he's a foghorn
we try to ignore.

Sometimes he's a goldfish
that the bear can't hold.
Sometimes he's the nails
through my mother's hands.

COMPANY

I don't tell them about the time you were supposed to pick me up from school or the payphone or the answering machine or how I walked home dragging my abandonment behind me like a limp dog. I don't tell them how it was the day before junior prom and we had plans—we were going to pick out a necklace to match my dress. I don't tell them how the front door was wide open, the dining room chairs passed out on the floor. How I carried a knife upstairs as if I was brave enough to use it. Don't tell them how I saw you on your bed and I thought that you were dead. How I lifted your forearms to see if you finally opened them. That I knew to check for your pulse because it was something I saw in a movie once. How the red hair stuck to your sweaty forehead—a river of blood. The bottle. The pills. I don't tell them how my brother's pictures were a quilt of grief around you. How we left the door unlocked in case he ever came home. I don't tell them how my voice hollowed when I called my father. How he waited in the car outside the jewelry store while I grabbed any old necklace off the shelf muttering, *This one, this one's fine.* When new company comes over, I tell them, *My mom is great—can't wait for you to meet her. What? Oh no, it's just me. I'm an only child.*

When I Noticed

This morning she tried to slice
a banana into my cereal, but fed me
a bowl full of thumbs.

When she dropped me at school
her lips stuck to my cheek. She drove off,
forgetting her mouth.

When I came home she'd left
a leg on the couch in front
of the television,

her tongue flopping on the countertop,
curled around a prescription pill.
A lone breast floating in the bathtub.

I followed a trail of molars
up the stairs. When she noticed me,
her head fell to the polished wood floor.

She swept it up, screwed
it back on—a light
she pretended was not flickering.

She smiled, wiped
a smudge from my face,
said,
> *oh, sweetie, look*
> *at this*
> > *mess.*

The Closet

I was a mischievous child. I told Briana I possessed a rare ruby she could only see in the dark, then lead her into my closet where my cat had birthed kittens once, licked them free from their gooey, eggplant-colored sacks. Briana was gullible. I once convinced her to eat cat food from my baby doll's plastic spoon. It was innocent enough. But when the closet door clicked behind us, I knew we were swallowed by the dark. We kicked the door like a bully's giant shin, clawing with the small voices of lace and pink girls. We missed the world of milk-dipped cookies, video games and kickball, even the cough of chalk dust. But no one ever heard us calling. So we turned twenty-five in that closet. Ended up skipping high school, which we heard was awful anyway. When we grew hungry, we ate my tiny balled up socks and I played the glockenspiel on Briana's protruding ribs. Eventually we married. We were the brides and the maids of honor, the flower girls too. We forgot the color of sunlight so we made up rumors about it. Once a year (I think) we'd try to open the door, just to see, but it never budged. So we never fell in love and we never got hurt. The planes crashed, the towers fell—we knew none of it. The princess in England we loved so much died in every home but ours. My dresses hung above us like ghosts of little girls. We are still angry at our mothers, who never found us. We wonder if they even tried.

JUMPER

When I hear her baking pies after midnight, rearranging the furniture, filling up the bathtub until it almost bubbles over, I know she's avoiding the spot in her bed that's next to my dad. I'm good at pretending to be asleep. An expert. I do it when she comes into my room and packs my suitcase. I do it in the morning when she carries me into the backseat of the car where there are pillows and lots of blankets. My brother has his headphones in, something spinning in his Walkman. He reclines the front seat all the way down and I trace his hair with my little toes. *We're going on an adventure!* she says. I like adventures because they usually mean I miss school. Sometimes she calls adventures *Mental Health Days*, and we sit in a dark movie theatre or get our toes painted. But today it's Niagara Falls, which is in Canada. It's a long drive and on the way we stop overnight in a museum of stained glass. It's like a church without God. My brother and I sit on a bench and play *Slaps*, a game where you try to slap the other person's hands real fast. *No flinching,* my brother says, while mom wanders the museum alone. The next day we wake up early and go to the waterfall. My mother stares, like she's watching a sad movie that my brother and I can't see. I don't know how long I'm supposed to look at a waterfall for. Not much happens. There's water. It falls. I learned the word *self-explanatory* last week and I use it all the time now. I'm seven. I also like the word *actually*. My brother prefers *whatever*. I think it's his favorite, like pizza. Waterfalls are pretty boring but the guide tells us that even though you can go to jail for it, some people tuck themselves away in a barrel and roll off the cliffs. An old lady did it once and she survived, but pretty much everyone dies. *That's actually crazy,* I say. My brother says his other favorite thing, *I'm bored,* and we tell mom we want to go back to the hotel and jump on the beds. *Later,* she says, with the kind of smile you get when the lemonade needs more sugar. When we lose her in the gift shop, my brother starts calling her name. But I don't. I run to the barrels.

PEARL

I'm in preschool!
There's a single pearl skating
down the linoleum floor—
and I gotta have it.
It's a loose rabbit
I'm gonna chase and shove
in my pockets—except
I don't have pockets.
But I do have nostrils
and pop! I've got a pearl
in my nose.
I've just robbed a bank.
I'm a three-year-old bandit,
giggling in my Mary Janes.
Until my teachers spot it.
They want to take the pearl.
It's the only game at recess: Fetch
The Pearl From Megan's Nose.
But they can't get it.
Only my mother's pinky, smaller
than all the Q-tips in the world,
can fish it out.
She tells me when she was little,
a mothball buried itself in her nose
because she liked how it smelled,
and her mother was scared too.
She said, *Never put anything in your nose again,*
and oh! there's something about those seven words
that make me want to do it, always, again.
Like when I found the tiny Ziploc
in my brother's coat pocket
whispered with white.
Or at the Halloween party
with the credit card and the mirror
and the bill rolled up like a telescope.

How she said, *Don't end up like me,*
before she left for the psych ward
and on the drive home
I pulled the car over
and got out
by the bridge.

APRIL 15, 2013

On his 31st birthday, my brother calls and tells me not to worry,
but our mother just admitted herself into the psych ward.
I wonder if this is her tiny gift to him—to lock up her sharp edges
in a padded room. To win the Mental Illness Olympics so he won't
feel bad that she's still paying his rehab bills and he's been drinking again.
I'm in an airport leaving New York. In the air, I don't think
about the plane crashing so much as never landing.
I call the flight attendant and make up things to want.
I push a button and she answers. See? Life is easy.
A stranger picks me up in the airport to drive me to the city
where they'll give me a microphone and an audience
and I'll talk about everything but this. The stranger
turns on the radio and when her sleeve falls back
I see the fresh cuts up her arm.
I want to believe they came from a dog
I know she doesn't have. And if I can't wish that
she never made the cuts, I wish that her sleeve
never shifted, that the wounds didn't smile their red smiles
at me as if to say, *We will follow you your whole life.*
The radio interrupts the things I don't say
to tell us that the marathon runners back in Boston
were greeted with bombs at the finish line.
The word *terrorism* comes back like a decade-late boomerang.
In a New York psych ward, my mother has a shadow
in white scrubs that follows her into the bathroom to make sure
she doesn't flush herself away. In Boston, her birthplace is exploding.
It's Tax Day and a few hours before I filed for an extension
to say, *I can't handle this now. Try again in six months.*
And see? Life is easy. When I no longer want to listen
to the rising tally of those injured anymore,
to the catalog of gruesome amputations, I turn
the channel to a sticky pop song and roll down the window.
See? Life is easy. The way blood leaving the body is easy.
The way taking the wheel from the stranger
and cutting it into the river below us is easy.
Just a small movement of muscle
and a pinch of bravery. The way lying is easy.
See? I'm doing it right now.

RETRACTION

in fear of my mother being diagnosed with Alzheimer's Disease

I knew it finally came for you
when I got the phone call—you'd forgotten
which street our house was on.
You were parked outside someone else's life,
car still running.

For years you'd call me
by my brother's name, or the cat's,
and eventually the name of your mother—
dead long before I was born.

Most days I have to tell you things fifty times:
Mom, you're okay.
Mom, I love you.
Mom, they're not trying to kill you.
Mom, I am your daughter. The only one.
Mom, this—this is your home now.

I think of all the questions I should have asked
before. I want to pull the answers from your mouth,
each memory a hair caught in the back of your throat.

If I could do it all again, I would do it all again.
I'd set the table at all the dinners I missed.
Come back for the Mother's Days I spent in other states.
I'd shift the finger hovering over the ignore button
and answer your call.

Mom, this is a fork.
Mom, you use it like this.
Mom, you can't leave the oven on.
Mom, September.
I love you. Annie.
Annie's your name.

When you tremble at the food
I am trying to spoon into your mouth,
I wonder if you see me as I was then: the girl
who accidentally caught your skin

in the sweater's zipper.
The girl who snuck out of windows
and stole your pills.

If you remember the time I slammed the door
so hard it sounded like *I hate you*
and the photograph of us fell off its nail.

Mom, he's been dead for years.
Mom, he loved you so much.
Mom, he's gone forever. Do you hear me? Forever.
Mom, he'll be back in five minutes.
Mom, he just went to the store.

I don't know how to live with these things
I've done—the secrets of yours I told
because of how they made me interesting—
this hurt I polished until I could see my own face in it.

Mom, you were a good woman.
Mom, you are a good woman.
Mom, look at all the people who love you.
Mom, they visit while you're sleeping.
Mom, all of them.

Now I know when you call me
on my birthday and say that the day
I was born, August 6th, 1988,
9:20AM, was the most magnificent day
of your life—I know

there were eighty years
of things to remember,
and you chose this.

When the building of your memory
went up in flames—
you saved this.

I.

GLUTTON

She's arranging flowers when I ask about their first date. *Spring, 1980,* she says, cutting the stems and running them under cold water. *The street was lined with cherry blossoms.* My eyes widen and she knows I want to hear it—the poetry. *The birds came back,* she continues, *and the ice cream truck trumpeted its anthem, luring children away from their baseball diamonds. The neighborhood kids chased after it, waving their allowance money like the tongues of thirsty dogs.* He called me his Redhead, she smiles, her teeth a row of wedding cakes. She adds flower food to the vase, tells me, *There was this chubby boy in the park, his tummy poked out between a striped shirt and khaki shorts that didn't exactly meet. He chirped his order: a double cone, swirled, rainbow sprinkles, cherry-dipped.* A thorn pricks her finger, she brings it to her lips. *The ice cream fell to the street,* she continues, *then Bob*—*your father*—she studies the arrangement, silent. *He said*—*well, he bent down to the boy and told him he didn't need it. Poked his stomach and laughed.* She fusses with a daisy and I can tell she still hears that laugh, still hears him call her *Redhead* instead of her mother-given name. *We were married within the year,* she tells me. I can tell she still thinks about the boy sometimes, wondering if he skips dessert or pool party invitations, or dates with pretty girls. I tell her, *Mom, he's okay.* I don't tell her how I know. The boy lives inside me. I will always feed him. *Look at all that chocolate on your face,* I tell him, *Who's going to love you now?*

THE DANCE CLASS

After the divorce, I spent more time in the dance studio
than I did with my father. Six hours a week bloodying my toes
after school. With each pirouette I unravelled

what awaited me at home.
During one of our court-sanctioned dinners,
my dad asked what I wanted for Christmas.

Well, Mom's already getting me an extra dance class,
I bragged. *Jazz.* I wanted him to know
what a good woman she was,

to hang a halo of mistletoe over her head
and parade her around him. For them to pick up their love again
as if it were a hobby, like knitting.

My father stuffed
a forkful into his mouth,
nodded.

A decade later, I learn the story
about the message left on his answering machine
from the night before, my mother's voice

caught in a plastic hell: *Megan wants a fourth dance class.*
You're gonna have to pay three quarters of it.
And you know what? You're a deadbeat dad.

His new wife begged him
to erase the message, he refused, stayed
up every night stabbing himself with it.

You're a deadbeat dad, rewind, *you're a deadbeat dad,*
rewind, *you're a deadbeat dad,* rewind,
you're a dead—

If you didn't know what she was saying
it would have been a sweet image,
a man who keeps his former wife's voice

on loop and cries into his big hands.
Or a girl, dancing in the studio, spinning
like a plastic ballerina freed from her music box,

dancing like she could put out the fire of this world
with her feet, leaping through the air
as if the love that made her still ran hot

through her every muscle,
not knowing
who would really pay for it.

PHOTOGRAPH OF MY PARENTS ON THEIR WEDDING DAY, 1980

The bride is flawless as an actress,
wears a wide-brimmed hat she can conceal
her jaded blue eyes beneath. Her lace dress
buttons to the throat.

A beard covers most of the groom's face.
Crooked bow tie suggests his hands shook while knotting it.
The boutonnière pinned to his lapel looks more like a firework
than a flower, exploding above his heart.

I want to say they were pressed together, lovesick teenagers
sharing a single diner booth—but no. They are in two
distinct, separate chairs. Another man
could fit between them.

Neither smile. They just stare
into their champagne, as if at the bottom
of their glasses they see a tremor of some future:
one where she miscarries,

rushes home to tell him, and he looks
at the delicate spot above her shoulder
where the football game continues to play,
pretends to listen.

CONCEPTION

She is alone on an empty train
when a tall stranger points to the seat beside her

and asks if it's taken.
It's a free country, she says,

my father sits down.
He pulls laughter from her

like a rabbit from a magician's hat.
This is all it takes.

Soon he will propose, a diamond
in a bucket of Cracker Jack.

She will blink six times.
It will mean *yes.*

For some time this will be enough.
He will lend her half his face for the boy.

Six years later, the other half for a daughter
who will watch her in the mirror.

She will rinse the last of his dishes.
Will take up Yoga. Reflexology. Learn Italian.

Zydeco dancing. He will always be the same
man he promised on their wedding day.

The tall stranger. The magician.
Even when she's stopped laughing.

Even when she's filled the empty seats beside her
with museums. Mountains. Downward-facing dog.

Book groups. Self-help sections of libraries.
I'm sorry, that seat is taken, she'll tell him.

No, you can't sit down.

Retraction To "Conception"

He didn't propose
with a ring in a bucket
of Cracker Jack.

Or, he did,
but to his first wife, Janet,
who was kept secret

in dusty photo albums
for twelve years.
I am a writer

because my father
spent all his romance
in one place.

     Here, my mother
     gets the Cracker Jack
     but swallows the ring.

     Here, my father
     is a fisherman.
     He casts a line

     down her throat and reels in
     an infant made of sugar.
     Here, she is enough

     to keep them together.
     She is the first baby
     never to cry.

THE HOTTEST DAY IN AUGUST, 1988

Pulling up to the hospital in a taxi,
my father steals the nearest wheelchair
and drops my mother in it. Her house dress
is floral and wet and she's fanning herself
with the crossword she was
just about to finish when—
my father is wheeling her, fast, the scrubs
and stethoscopes and coughs whizzing by
like trees outside a speeding car. My father calls
for a doctor, their doctor,
tells him about the castor oil. The puddle.
Mom paces the small, bright room
in paper slippers, exhaling like a puffer fish
on display in one of those China Buffet tanks
that I'll later spend the second half of Christmases
with Dad staring through.

They inspect and measure how far she's opened,
the doctors tuning into the radio of her body
and judging its traffic. They lay her on her back, legs up
in the air, in a position that looks remarkably
similar to my making, and tell her to push.
My father says, *Breathe, Bunny.*
He's a good coach, and one day he'll prove it
by managing my softball team or banging his big hands
together after I read a poem in a seedy bar.
He wipes a sweaty ribbon of hair from her forehead
and I wish I was born already so I could see it. This love
that made me. This love I'll destroy.
No one knows it will be the last time.

ACKNOWLEDGMENTS

The author would like to thank the publications who graciously gave homes to the following poems first:

The Collagist — The Third Ceremony

Germ Magazine — Ashley Handler Doesn't Walk, She Floats; Company; Cutting School

Mobius — Backhanded Apology

MUZZLE Magazine — Cinnamon and Sand

The Orange Room Review — Anything for You; Conception

Radius — Alibi; K; Telling Him I Kissed a Woman

The Rattling Wall — Glutton; Tutor

Uncommon Core — Golden Boy; What We Lose

Union Station Magazine — Pearl

Words Dance — Safelight

Tremendous love and gratitude to Jeanann Verlee, Sean Patrick Mulroy, and Jared Singer for their editing, friendship, and belief in this book. Angel Nafis for her *In Real Life* writing workshop which excavated some of these poems from a secret well inside. April Ranger for her wonder and for lending me *The Gold Cell* by Sharon Olds, which gave me permission for truth. Chelsea Coreen for being the glitteriest intern and the first pair of wide eyes on most of these poems. Derrick Brown for his dream-weaving and impossibly magical brain. Miles Walser for his time spilled into making this book, and me, better. Sean, Bob, and Annie Falley, for raising me to be a poet, for making me the keeper of these beautiful and gruesome stories.

ABOUT MEGAN FALLEY

Megan Falley is the nationally touring author of *Redhead and the Slaughter King* and *After the Witch Hunt*, both realeased by Write Bloody Publishing. She has performed her work on television as a part of TV One's *Verses and Flow*. Winner of their chapbook contest, Falley's book *Bad Girls, Honey* (Poems about Lana Del Rey), is slated for publication with Tired Hearts Press. Falley was a finalist at both the National Poetry Slam and the Women of the World Poetry Slam in 2014. She is the founder of the online writing course *Poems That Don't Suck*, and lives in a small zoo in Brooklyn. | MeganFalley.com |

IF YOU LOVE MEGAN FALLEY,
MEGAN FALLEY LOVES . . .

Drunks & Other Poems of Recovery
by Jack McCarthy

This Way to the Sugar
by Hieu Nguyen

What the Night Demands
by Miles Walser

Racing Hummingbirds
by Jeanann Verlee

Glitter in the Blood: A Guide to Braver Writing
by Mindy Nettifee

Write Bloody Publishing distributes and promotes great books of fiction, poetry, and art every year. We are an independent press dedicated to quality literature and book design, with an office in Austin, TX.

Our employees are authors and artists, so we call ourselves a family. Our design team comes from all over America: modern painters, photographers, and rock album designers create book covers we're proud to be judged by.

We publish and promote 8 to 12 tour-savvy authors per year. We are grass-roots, D.I.Y., bootstrap believers. Pull up a good book and join the family. Support independent authors, artists, and presses.

Want to know more about Write Bloody books, authors, and events?
Join our mailing list at

www.writebloody.com

WRITEBLOODY
QUALITY AMERICAN BOOKS

WRITE BLOODY BOOKS

The Importance of Being Ernest — Ernest Cline

In Search of Midnight — Mike McGee

The Incredible Sestina Anthology — Daniel Nester, Editor

Junkyard Ghost Revival anthology

Kissing Oscar Wilde — Jade Sylvan

The Last Time as We Are — Taylor Mali

Learn Then Burn — Tim Stafford and Derrick C. Brown, Editors

Learn Then Burn Teacher's Manual — Tim Stafford and Molly Meacham, Editors

Learn Then Burn 2: This Time It's Personal — Tim Stafford, Editor

Live For A Living — Buddy Wakefield

Love in a Time of Robot Apocalypse — David Perez

The Madness Vase — Andrea Gibson

Multiverse: An anthology of Superhero Poetry of Superhuman Proportions —
Rob Sturma & Ryk Mcintyre

The New Clean — Jon Sands

New Shoes On A Dead Horse — Sierra DeMulder

No Matter the Wreckage — Sarah Kay

Oh, Terrible Youth — Cristin O'Keefe Aptowicz

The Oregon Trail Is The Oregon Trail — Gregory Sherl

Our Poison Horse — Derrick C. Brown

Over the Anvil We Stretch — Anis Mojgani

The Pocketknife Bible — Anis Mojgani

Pole Dancing to Gospel Hymns — Andrea Gibson

Racing Hummingbirds — Jeanann Verlee

Redhead and The Slaughter King — Megan Falley

Rise of the Trust Fall — Mindy Nettifee

Scandalabra — Derrick C. Brown

Slow Dance With Sasquatch — Jeremy Radin

The Smell of Good Mud — Lauren Zuniga

Songs from Under the River — Anis Mojgani

Spiking the Sucker Punch — Robbie Q. Telfer